DARK PSYCHOLOGY

Discover The Art Of Reading And Analyzing People

BENEDICT GOLEMAN

Table of Contents

INTRODUCTION

Congratulations on purchasing ***Dark Psychology*** and thank you for doing so.

Have you ever wondered why some of the most insidious people on the planet are somehow able to charm everyone to fall for their every whim? Think of serial killers like Ted Bundy—he was commonly believed to be a handsome, charismatic young man that was able to quickly and easily win the favor of others almost naturally, and yet behind the scenes, he was a serial rapist and murderer of at least 30 homicides over a 4 year period of time. How did he do it? How was he able to sneak past so many people undetected for so long?

The answer is through dark psychology.

Many of the darkest personality types out there are quite capable of seeming charming and affable, only to be hiding the monster underneath their masks. This is a method they use to prey on other people, victimizing those who dare to fall for their charm. Dark psychology delves into these personality types, studying the underlying motivations for the behaviors at hand. This is not only to understand what to look out for when you are in the real world—when you learn to understand the minds of those with dark personalities, you can begin to claim their own ways of thinking.

Dark psychology is a study of people with these dark personalities, but also a study of the tactics that are used, why they work, and how they can be adapted. You can use several of these tactics without becoming abusive or using them in a harmful way. What if you were able to find ways to come across as charming and persuasive to others, and you used those powers to help yourself and others? Perhaps you, being charismatic and particularly skilled in influence, were able to become a powerful leader within a company—you could use the powers of dark psychology to keep morale up, keep people motivated, and ensure that others are happy and willing to move forward. You would be able to always find the perfect way to convince other people to carry on. You would be able to ensure that everyone under your charge was happy to help. You would find yourself running a particularly successful business.

Now, what if you were in sales or politics and convincing people is what you need to do best? Dark psychology can show you the ways that people are able to slip undetected into the mind of another to plant ideas, convince others to see things your way, and move forward. You could use these skills in advertising or consulting. Despite the root in darkness and evil, dark psychology techniques can be particularly useful, even under the most innocent contexts, and this book seeks to show you exactly how they are able to do that.

This book will guide you through an overview of dark psychology, allowing you to get to know those dark personality types and how they work. You will learn about manipulation and how to use it to control the minds of others. You will learn to persuade with skill. You will understand the insidiousness of brainwashing and how it can be used to completely indoctrinate a person into a certain belief system. You will discover deception and neuro-linguistic processing. You will learn to use hypnosis to coax people into a state of suggestibility. Lastly, you will see the benefits of dark psychology, learning how it can be used in daily relationships in order to help all involved.

There are plenty of books on this subject on the market, thanks again for choosing this one! Every effort was made to ensure it is full of as much useful information as possible, please enjoy!

CHAPTER 1: DARK PSYCHOLOGY

Psychology at its root is something that is relatively simple to define—it is the scientific study of the mind. It covers several different aspects, looking into relationships, behaviors, thought processes, and more. When you are looking into psychology, you are looking for the why and how of essentially any human process form the mental side. You may be looking at neurobiological processes, such as what happens within the brain when it is actively controlling the body, or you may be looking at why that 5-year-old child at the grocery store had a massive meltdown when told no to candy. It studies all of that and more, but essentially, it is the study of who we are as a species and as an individual. It studies what we do, what drives us, and what causes us problems. It explains emotions and how they both function and aid humans in acting. It explains why some people give in to pressure, but others do not. It explains why empathy is so important.

Ultimately, psychology exists in several different classifications. Some people are only interested in the physical aspect while others care about development. Others still are interested in the divergences between typical psychological development and the developments of people who may become particularly hard to live with. It has several uses, both practical and simply intellectual—if you understand human psychology, you are able to see and predict how people will behave. Knowing those tendencies, you can accurately figure out what will happen, and learn how to use those tendencies to your own benefit.

Defining Dark Psychology

Dark psychology, in particular, will look specifically at the psychology of people that have a very specific personality type. In particular, we are looking at those who are Machiavellian, narcissistic, sadistic, and psychopathic. These people tend to be among the most dangerous that you can encounter, and they will have no qualms about using and abusing other people. However, there is much to learn from this personality type—if you can come to understand this personality type and the tactics that are commonly used, you will be able to emulate them without the threat or harm that may otherwise go along with them.

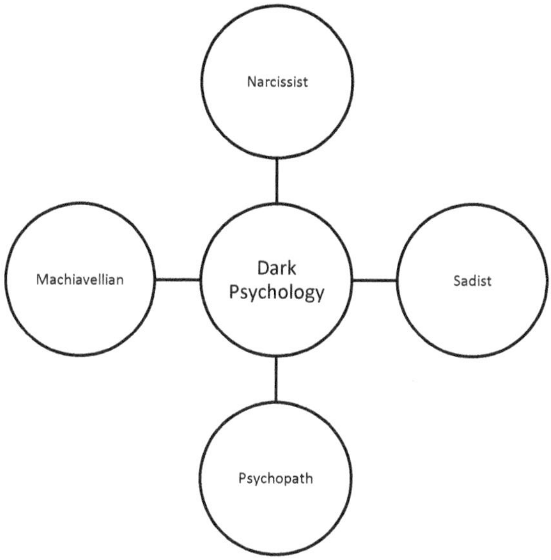

In particular, this book will be looking at the behaviors of those with dark personality types. We will spend Chapter 2 looking specifically at the dark side of psychology, studying what those particular personality traits are and how they present themselves. From there, the duration of the book will be spent studying the behavior of those specific personality types.

Dark psychology assumes that when people behave in abusive manners, using techniques like manipulation and deception, it almost always has a reason. We will look at those reasons and applications as well, learning what it is that makes these tools so attractive to monsters in human clothing that are willing to wield them. You will see exactly why people behave in ways that are abusive or evil, how they come to the realization that they do that justifies the abuse in their minds, and how they are able to overcome the empathy and compassion that usually prevents people from behaving in such abusive manners.

We will look at several of the most commonly used techniques of the abusive personality types, and from there, we will spend time discussing how several of them can be used in a wider context, allowing for their usages during day-to-day interactions. Instead of manipulating someone to abuse them, you can look into how to use the same skills to help persuade and guide people toward whatever they need to do.

We will also look into how these particular tactics impact the person that is being subjected to them. Some of these techniques work through instilling feelings in other people, knowing that emotions are incredibly motivating. Others work through accessing the unconscious mind, suggesting certain behaviors. Others still work through acts of deception.

Understanding dark psychology will not only enable you to understand the actions of personality types such as the narcissist, the Machiavellian, and the psychopath but also be able to combat it. You will be able to avoid falling for their tactics if you know what the tactics are. This means that learning to think like the darkest personality types is imperative—when you can think like them, you can identify them.

The History of Dark Psychology

Traditionally considered a field of applied psychology, dark psychology begins with the study of the dark triad or the study of manipulation. Considering that dark personality types have existed as long as history can record, it comes as no surprise that those interested in understanding these dark types have been scattered across history as well. In particular, it is possible to find evidence of studies surrounding manipulation and abuse in nearly every culture around the world. Humans have always victimized other humans as long as they have been able to. You can read in history books about how people used to take slaves, destroy other towns and villages, and steal.

Ultimately, up until relatively recently in history, attempts to manipulate and control other people were common, but not particularly controlled or recorded. It happened on a regular basis, but without proper guidance and logging that allows for it to be tracked. After all, even religious texts make reference to manipulation, such as referencing Eve being deceived by the snake.

In proper psychology, there have been studies to determine how stimulations of any kind can change behaviors. These have studied aspects such as whether fear can be conditioned and learned, or whether adding certain situations or wording could convince people to act in certain ways.

Perhaps one of the earliest records of controlling the behaviors of others comes in 1897 with Ivan Pavlov's study of dogs and their behavior. He learned that some of the behavior of dogs seems to be innate, such as salivating in response to food. He also learned that innate behaviors can be linked to other stimuli. Instead of the dog salivating at food, for example, he conditioned the dogs to salivate to the sound of a bell through what was eventually called classical conditioning.

In classical conditioning, you are able to take unconditioned responses and cause them with unconditioned stimuli. The food is the unconditioned stimulus, and in response to seeing it, the dog will salivate in response. That unconditioned stimulus gets paired with a conditioned stimulus, and in response over time, you will see that the unconditioned response occurs when exposed to the conditioned stimulus.

The concept of classical conditioning was strongly supported by psychologist John Watson, who declared that he believed that classical conditioning was involved in all aspects of human development and psychology. He pushed the point in 1920 in an experiment during which he conditioned a 9-month-old infant to fear anything white and fuzzy.

In particular, during this experiment, a child referred to as Little Albert was provided access to several white animals in a neutral setting. He was shown a rat, a rabbit, a monkey, and several other items. At first, Little Albert was not afraid of any of them. He was unafraid of what he saw in front of him. Eventually, the white rat was presented, along with the sudden loud bang of a hammer on a steel bar just behind his head. While the rat itself was not disturbing to the child, the sound was, and he cried. From 11 months on, he was exposed to the rat with the loud noise occurring once a week for seven weeks. Of course, the child cried each time. After the seven weeks, all that researchers had to do to trigger the meltdown was to show him the rat in question. Upon seeing the rat, even without the noise, he would cry in fear and attempt to flee.

That was not all—Little Albert became phobic of anything that was white and fuzzy. Whether a white dog, a piece of cotton wool or even Santa Claus, the sight of something white and fuzzy was enough to send him into a panic. While this behavioral response faded somewhat over time without reinforcement, it was still readily triggered by repeating the creation of the loud sound that went along with the rat.

This becomes a foundation for many different forms of manipulation and influence. You will see this concept arise repeatedly when you look at neuro-linguistic programming, during which you will see what is called anchoring, a technique to trigger a certain behavior with a specific emotional response. It can also be relevant in emotional manipulation as well.

After the discovery and conceptualization of classical conditioning, the concept of operant conditioning arose as well. Particularly in 1936, B.F Skinner came up with the concept, drawing heavily from Thorndike's 1898 Law of Effect, which posited that anything with a positive consequence is likely to be repeated, while anything with a negative consequence is going to be avoided. For example, if a child is given a piece of candy after cleaning up his mess, the child is going to be more inclined to pick up the toys in the future, thanks to the positive effect. Conversely, if the child yells at someone and then gets a negative consequence, such as having to go to their room, they are not as likely to repeat it.

This concept was reiterated within Skinner's theory, and he added to it a new concept—reinforcement. Skinner asserted that if a behavior is reinforced, meaning that it is rewarded, it will be repeated or strengthened. The person is likely to repeat those behaviors that are reinforced because they had a good result. However, when reinforcement does not occur, that behavior is going to be weakened or extinguished.

In 1948, Skinner reiterated these concepts with experiments. He created what he called a "*Skinner Box*" which was a box in which an animal had access to a lever, a speaker, and two signal lights. There was also an electrical grid on the bottom that would generate a shock. The animals were shocked when they pressed the lever with a specific light illuminated, but when they used the lever with the other light illuminated, they were rewarded with a piece of food.

Through this experiment, it was shown that there are three types of responses that will follow a behavior: Neutral operands, during which the environment neither encourages nor discourages the repetition of behavior, reinforcers, which drive the individual to repeat the behavior and punishers, which discourage the repetition.

You will see this concept when looking at techniques such as intermittent reinforcement, during which a manipulator will give positive reinforcement only sometimes. As you can see, much of behaviorism becomes incredibly relevant to the study of dark psychology.

The 1960s came with Albert Bandura, another prominent behaviorist, acknowledging and agreeing with classical and operant conditioning while also adding two distinct and important ideas. He asserted that there are processes between the stimuli exposed to and responses and that behavior is a learned concept that develops via observational learning.

In particular, Bandura presented an experiment known as the Bobo doll experiment in 1961. He argued that children, in particular, will pay attention to the behaviors or their models—people that they are surrounded by—and they will imitate the behaviors that they were exposed to. Think of how a toddler may yell out something embarrassing in public, not realizing that it is embarrassing because he has heard it from his parents: This is the perfect example.

In Bandura's experiment, he exposed children between the ages of 3 and 6 to violent behaviors toward a doll. First, children were studied to see how aggressive they were as a baseline. They were then sorted into groups of similar temperaments, in which some were shown an aggressive role model, some were shown a non-aggressive role model, and some were given no role model. The aggressive role model was aggressive toward a Bobo doll—they were given a hammer to beat the doll with and threw the doll around while yelling, "Pow, boom!" The non-aggressive model saw a model ignoring the doll and playing with another toy quietly.

The children were then offered access to several other toys, which a researcher told them were the best toys of all. Their behaviors were then recorded. Children who had been exposed to the aggressive behaviors tended to behave aggressively toward the Bobo doll that they had access to. This shows us that children learn behaviors through observation—social behavior is learned and influenced heavily based upon model, becoming the basis for the Social Learning Theory.

This is further supported in several of the tactics used in dark psychology as well. People are more readily persuaded by people similar to them, much like how the children are more likely to mimic people similar to them. People are also more likely to mimic others in unfamiliar settings as well, which is displayed in tactics such as persuasion.

As you continue to read through this book, you will find that much of the concepts that are innately used by the manipulators that are being studied involve many of the concepts of behaviorism. It becomes recurring, and in a way, it makes sense: Behaviorism is a study of how people act and how the environment influences behavior. Dark psychology seeks to control and change the behaviors of other people. As you continue to read, keep these key processes in mind as they will be quite relevant.

CHAPTER 2: THE DARK SIDE OF PERSONALITY

Imagine Anna for a moment: Young, finishing up her last year at college, and single. She is out with friends at a bar, and her other two friends have both already met people that they are animatedly chatting with. Anna, however, is a bit more self-conscious. She does not feel like she belongs there, and she sits between her friends, sipping at her drink. Then, she sees him.

The man is handsome and smiling at her. He approaches and offers to buy her a drink. He says his name is Ethan and that he has just graduated from the same university Anna goes to, just last year. He asks a few questions that are not too prying—is she a student? What is she studying? What a coincidence—he also majored in business! Is she from the area? No way—he grew up 30 minutes from her hometown. They seem like normal questions to Anna—he is getting to know her, and it appears that they have several major things in common. She chats with him, and soon, they are talking about her past relationship and how it was incredibly messy, so she isn't looking for anything at the moment.

Instead of scaring him away, he nods sagely and acknowledges that he had been in a relationship with a particularly abusive, narcissistic woman not too long ago and he was just looking for someone to get to know as friends. They spend the rest of the night in the bar chatting happily, and when Anna and her friends are ready to go, he smiles, writes down his phone number for her, and bids them good night.

Anna finds herself hooked—she cannot stop thinking about Ethan and how much they had in common. Soon, she is texting him, and she finds out that not only have their lives paralleled quite closely, they share very similar hobbies. They both like to sit in and read with a nice cup of wine. They both like to go on hikes in the nearby mountains. They both share a love for playing video games—but the same type of obscure RPG, not the mainstream titles that come out.

Soon, Ethan has slid into Anna's life entirely. He is over at her apartment 5 or 6 days a week and stays the night at least half of them, usually falling asleep halfway through a movie. He brings her flowers and lavishes her in positive attention. He loves to listen for hours about everything that she has gone through in the last few years and offer his own opinions as someone who had been in a similar relationship before.

Anna tells herself that he is the one. He is different. He is kind and caring. He knows how to listen. She soon finds herself head over heels in love with him. They fall hard and fast for each other, and within three months, they are engaged—after all, they are soul mates. Six months later, she is pregnant.

Nine months later, they are married. Shortly before the baby is born, it is like a switch has flipped. He is mean and cold. He is constantly disappearing overnight at the bar. He puts her down and when she cries, he calls her hormonal. It was like the Ethan that she knew, loved, and married, was nothing but a lie.

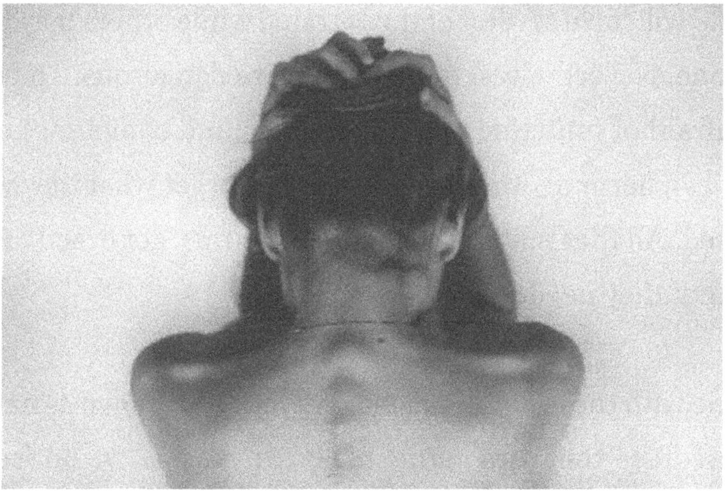

This is because he *had* lied. People with dark personalities have no qualms about preying on other people. Just as the wolf does not think twice about the feelings of deer, the dark personality type does not care about his victims. Ethan had disguised himself precisely *because* he was hunting Anna: He was intentionally trying to make himself attractive to her—

he wanted to be able to interest and attract her in order to gain control.

Oftentimes, people with dark personalities, with the propensity to manipulate, hunt, and use other people, present themselves in four different ways: They are Machiavellian, narcissistic, sadistic, or psychopathic. Some people will have several of these traits, while others may have just one. Nevertheless, these people are dangerous. They are not afraid of inflicting extreme mental, and sometimes even physical, harm to other people in order to get what they want or need. All that matters to them is that they get exactly what it is that they needed.

People with these dark personality types are known as having dark cores—they are more likely to engage in antisocial behaviors such as behaving malevolently, stealing, cheating, or hurting other people. These are the people engaging in dark psychology, and the more that you read through the book, the more you will come to recognize the methods through which these personality types choose to act.

Within this chapter, we will stop and take a look at four of the darkest personality types—we will look at the Machiavellian, the narcissist, the psychopath, and the sadist. We will go over the classical presentation of each of these personality traits, as well as the motivators for each. While each of them is their own distinct type, with very specific traits, they all share similarities. In particular, each of these dark personality types lacks empathy.

A Note on Empathy

Empathy is the ability to understand and feel other people's emotions. It is primarily responsible for facilitating communication between people, allowing others access to the emotional states of those around them. In particular, it allows for people to act compassionately—you can put yourself in someone else's shoes, so to speak. If you can see that the person across from you is stressed out, you can relate. You can feel that sort of stress yourself if you are particularly empathetic. In knowing the emotions of someone else, you can then feel moved to help—you can offer to do something to alleviate that stress.

In other instances, empathy allows for the regulation of your own behaviors. If you can empathize with someone else, you can make sure that you, yourself, are not the cause of their distress. Consider for a moment that you are talking to someone and say something that offends them. If you can empathize with them, you can see and understand that you upset them—and you actually care. In being able to acknowledge that you have upset them, you can then make it a point to change your own behaviors. This is why empathy is so critical, and why lacking it can be so dangerous. It is what usually acts as a deterrent to hurting other people needlessly.

Machiavellianism

The first of the personality traits that will be discussed is Machiavellianism. Machiavellians are people who are highly manipulative by nature—they are able to cheat people out of things without you ever knowing that it has happened. This particular trait is named for Niccolo Machiavelli—a diplomat and philosopher responsible for writing The Prince—a book that discussed that strong rulers must be harsh on their subjects in order to keep their rule. In particular, it is believed that the earning of glory and survival will justify any means. Effectively, then, this is the beginning of the flawed idea that the ends will always justify the means.

The people with this personality type, then, encompass that form of thinking. They feel that they can be manipulative with little repercussions, or that the repercussions are meaningless so long as they get their way.

The Machiavellian is focused on his or her own ambition—all that matters is success, no matter what the cost. They will always prioritize their own success, regardless of what their idea of success is. If they believe that success is defined by their income, they will maximize that income, no matter the cost, for example.

Of course, if they are willing to succeed at any cost, they are typically incredibly exploitative. They will have no issues with taking advantage of other people, their weaknesses, or even throwing people under the bus if they think that it will be enough to get them the success, they believe that they deserve. There is no such thing as going too far with the Machiavellian, so long as the Machiavellian gets his or her way at the end of the day.

These people tend to be incredibly calculating. They will constantly be acting in their own best interests, even when people do not think that they are. If they are kind and do a favor, it is because they know that doing that favor is the best way to ensure that the other party is going to give them what they want later. Nothing they do is without reason, and they are not likely to help other people unless they can see some sort of legitimate benefit to doing so. This makes it incredibly difficult to identify their true intentions.

The Machiavellian, despite coming across as charming and flattering, is usually incredibly cynical—he does not believe that anyone will ever do anything for reasons that are not self-serving. To the Machiavellian, if anyone does something nice to them, it is because they want or need something and think that being ice will get it. In reality, they lack the value of inherent human kindness that they typically take advantage of, and their lack of empathy means that they do not care when they are taking advantage of other people. They will actively and readily harm other people, making other people fall for them without ever really committing to legitimate relationships. However, because they are so skilled at reading those around them and deceiving other people, they are commonly seen as far more charismatic and caring than they actually are.

Narcissism

The narcissist, on the other and is far less intentional and calculating. While the Machiavellian is incredibly meticulous in his manipulation, narcissists do not make the intentional decision to be manipulative people. They also lack the empathy necessary to regulate their actions regarding how other people see them, but in terms of the motivations, the narcissist is manipulative because the narcissist is delusional.

The narcissists are particularly exhausting because they have their own grand sense of self—in fact, it is so grand, that most of the time, it is grandiose. They are completely convinced that they are the best people out there, and entirely perfect. Because they are so confident in their perfection, they effectively believe that they are right all the time. There is no way that they can be wrong because they believe that they cannot be flawed, and this turns into them believing that when there is a disconnect between what they expect to be true versus what is actually true, they tend to assume that their own beliefs are the ones that are right.

This gets incredibly exhausting as people deal with them—they believe that they are perfect and inherently deserving of more than those around them. They think that they deserve special treatment and consideration and that treatment and consideration means that they will do anything to get it.

Effectively, the narcissist's manipulation and harm toward others comes out of that expectation of being right all of the time, believing that their grandiosity is justification of everything. However, the problem with the narcissist is that he is so skilled in convincing other people that he is right and deserving of special treatment that he will even gaslight himself into believing it. The narcissist will absolutely believe his narrative of what happens. If he tells someone that something did not happen in a certain way, they have likely convinced themselves of that narrative to protect that image of perfection that they are so certain about. They will always believe that they are deserving of that perfection, no matter what.

Narcissists themselves crave the center of attention—while they are unable to empathize with other people, they absolutely believe that they are deserving of the adoration of others, and they require it in order to feel like they are justified. They have a constant need to be admired, and if they are not admired, they will do things to gain that admiration, even if it hurts other people.

Psychopathy

Of the four traits that we are looking at, psychopaths are quite arguably the worst of the four. These people have the greatest potential to be harmful. When attempting to identify their personality tendencies, the psychopath is someone who flags as highly callous, impulsive, manipulative, and grandiose.

Effectively, the psychopath is someone who is not afraid of hurting other people to get what he wants. He is willing to give in to those impulses that would usually be disregarded quickly. If he has the thought that he wants to hurt someone else or toy with someone's emotions, he will do so as a game, simply because he can. He believes that he is able to do this without regard for the feelings of other people, and he will do it without thinking twice.

Like the narcissist, the psychopath thinks incredibly highly of himself—he believes that he is smarter than other people and that he is skilled enough to get away with whatever he wants to do. If he decides that he will become a serial killer, he is convinced that no one will ever be able to catch him—he is entirely of the belief that he is more intelligent, sneakier, and more capable than any of the people who have attempted this manipulation before him.

Despite the monstrous nature of the psychopath, they are actually incredibly adept at social situations. Unlike the narcissist, who may struggle in social settings if his grandiosity gets the best of him, the psychopath is even more skilled at blending in. They are able to emulate normal humans with ease and will do so to their own advantage. They see their skill at blending in as a game and they will often try to convince as many people as possible that they are trustworthy in order to take advantage again later.

Sadism

While the previous three make up the personality types commonly referred to as the dark triad, there is one more trait that is important to consider here when discussing dark psychology—the sadist. The sadist has all of the callousness of the dark triad, but unlike them, they are not particularly impulsive or manipulative. The sadist is someone who is entirely motivated because he enjoys being cruel.

The everyday sadist simply wants to hurt people or watch people suffer. He may make it a point to join the military or police force, allowing himself to shield himself from any repercussions. Within those particular career paths, he may feel like he can hurt people or be exposed to harm of others without having to hide it.

Of course, if that sadism comes along with one of the other personality types, such as paired with narcissistic personality disorder, it can become incredibly problematic—the sadistic narcissist is one that genuinely enjoys hurting people but may even feel like he has a right to do so. He will be able to justify his actions without having to try very hard simply because he knows that he is better than other people.

Dark Personalities and Abuse

Ultimately, these personality types lend themselves to abusive individuals due to the increase in callousness when compared to the others. Because of the callousness, none of the people discussed in this chapter have any qualms about their abuse. This means that Ethan, in his relationship with Anna, does not care about the pain that has been inflicted. He does not care that he effectively trapped someone under false pretenses, creating an indelible bond between the two of them forever. Even if she were to leave, she would never be able to truly escape him thanks to the fact that they share a child.

Studies have been done on the dark personality types that have shown that these people will tend to choose to act in ways that inflict pain, especially if they are quite sadistic. In this study, people were asked to choose from one of several jobs—the study was disguised in order to make the participants believe that they were looking at personality type and job preference. The jobs were to reflect the type of dark behaviors that they would then be told to do. Some of the jobs were to work in the cold, work in sanitation, or being an exterminator.

Unsurprisingly, most of the sadists chose extermination. From there, the scientists created what they called a killing machine—a coffee grinder that was modified in order to make crunching sounds, and they were instructed that they had to kill several bugs in names with cute names in an attempt to humanize them. Throughout the experiment, the sadists absolutely did choose to kill the bugs, and they were not disgusted by it. They were happy to kill the bugs and enjoyed it, though compared to people without sadistic tendencies, they enjoyed anything that they chose to do less than their non-sadistic counterparts.

After these results, another experiment was performed—during this one, people were sorted based on personality, and then were asked to play a computer game. The people playing the game were told that they were competing in order to blast a loud noise at the people in the other room. If they won, they would be able to choose how long and loud the blast would be. As an important note, the opponents never blasted back.

Half of these people would then have to work to be cruel—if they won, they would then need to count before the blast of noise would occur, with the interest of the study being how likely the extra work would deter the people from being aggressive. Ultimately, only the sadists chose to work to hurt the other party. While those with the dark personality types would all inflict some degree of harm to the opponents when it was easy, adding the extra layer of work was enough to deter the other personality types. Beyond just that, the sadists also chose to raise the blast and make it longer just to hurt the other team when they realized that there would be no retaliation.

Effectively, then, the sadists are the ones who are more likely to hurt other people. Even the psychopaths, who will hurt or kill without feeling bad about it, usually had purpose to drive them. The Machiavellians were too calculating to risk the harm of other people unless they felt like the payoff was right. The narcissists usually went out of their way to hurt others when they were threatened. However, the sadists would hurt just to enjoy themselves.

This means that, at the end of the day, it is the sadists that are going to be the most manipulative. The narcissists will be aggressive and abusive in response to the perception of a threat to themselves or their ego. The psychopath will hurt to gain something or because he wants something. The

Machiavellian will abuse only when it seems like the best way to get what he wants, and it will not be risky to do so.

CHAPTER 3: DARK PSYCHOLOGY'S EFFECTS

Finally, you have arrived at the last chapter of *How to Analyze People with Dark Psychology*. This is where your journey of learning begins to wrap to a close. Nevertheless, it is critical for you to learn just a bit more about dark psychology and its effects before you move on. Remember, dark psychology is a potent tool that can be used to gain plenty of insight and intelligence, but at the same time, it can also be seen as a sort of weapon. People who do not know what they are doing may struggle to actively ensure that they avoid hurting other people, and unfortunately, when you are poking around in someone's mind, the damage that you can potentially do can be irrevocable in some situations, such as if you have inflicted some sort of trauma in your manipulation attempts.

Dark psychology may be designed to be a study and mimicry of those with the dark triad's most potent methods of manipulation, but that does not mean that the act of interacting with other people must be harmful or detrimental to anyone involved. On the contrary, you can use these techniques and your powers in ways that are ethical. You can choose to wield your tools in ways that are actually beneficial for everyone involved as opposed to using these dark psychology techniques simply to hurt other people and get whatever it was that you were craving or wanting.

When you are willing to use dark psychology with the intention of doing real good in the world, you may find that the techniques and tools take a different light. There may be some that you choose to avoid, but there could also be others that are quite compelling to you. For example, what if you made it a point to use mind control techniques, but instead of convincing the other person that she was not good enough or too loud for you, you boosted her confidence, reminding her of how capable and beautiful she was? Suddenly, that technique that used to be insidious is actually quite compassionate.

This chapter will serve to wrap everything up once and for all. Within this chapter, you will look at the harm that dark psychology can do to an individual. You will see several signs of manipulation and abuse. Then, you will be provided with an explanation of ethical dark psychology, as well as a brief guide to ensuring that your own usage remains ethical. Lastly, you will be shown several examples of dark psychology techniques being used in ways that are helpful and benevolent rather than harmful and destructive.

Ethical Dark Psychology

As the name implies, ethical dark psychology would be the usage of dark psychology in ways that are not implicitly harmful. Of course, many people may argue that dark psychology is wrong, no matter who uses it simply because it accesses one's mind, the most private part of one's self. Nevertheless, if you can keep your dark psychology ethical, you can find that you are actually doing plenty of good. That good energy that you put out into the world will help several people, and you never know just how far that ripple of one good deed will flow.

This section will address five questions that you can ask in order to determine whether you are harmful or malicious in your attempts to get results from other people.

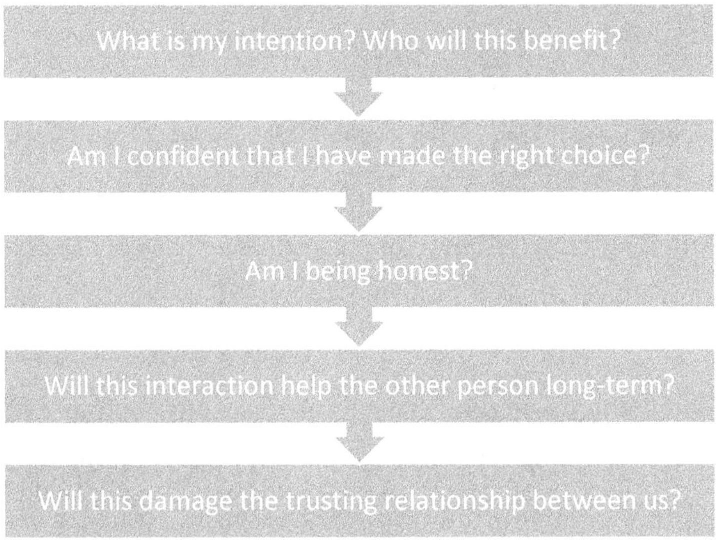

What is the intention of this interaction? Who will this benefit?

This question is the first one in the list—it is designed to make sure that whatever you are doing is not solely designed to benefit you. Remember, manipulators are those who tend to manipulate simply because they wish to take control of other people and serve themselves. When you are able to answer honestly that you have no interest in serving yourself but would rather see that other people are the ones benefitting, you are on the right track.

Am I confident that I am doing the right thing with this interaction?

This question forces you to figure out whether or not you are doing something that you truly believe is right or if you are doing something that you feel obligated to do or something that you know is ethically or morally ambiguous or simply wrong. When you can answer that you are, in fact, confident that you have chosen to do the right thing, no matter how you are approaching or interacting with someone else, then you can guarantee that you are actually going to be able to sleep with yourself. Remember, the true manipulators, the true ones that cause harm, do not care about this. They do not care that they are hurting people, so long as they get what they want.

Am I being honest here?

Now, this right here can eliminate several tactics from your repertoire that has been built up thus far if you are truly looking to remain ethical. However, you must make sure that you remember that people have their own free wills. You must be willing to respect that to ensure that you can actually make them happy or benefit them without assuming that they need someone there, holding their hand, and treating them like a baby that is incapable of caring for themselves. If you can do this effectively, you will be able to maintain their own autonomy.

Will this interaction benefit the other person in the long-term?

This once again causes you to look at whether or not your actions are beneficial to the other party. You need to make sure that what you have chosen to do is something that you are confident will help the other party; otherwise, who are you helping? Most likely, the only other option would be yourself, and you should not be using people as a means to an end.

Will my choice in method allow a relationship based on trust to develop?

This is the last question to ask yourself and is perhaps one of the most important. Will the way that you have chosen to influence the other person to damage your relationship with them, or will they still be able to trust you? Would they be able to trust you if you happened to tell them what you have done? If you have to feel like whatever you are doing must be hidden from the person that you are interacting with, it may be time to reconsider your tactics and what you seek to achieve. After all, you should not be making people feel like they do not get a say or like you think you know better than they do about what they want or need.

Signs of Manipulation

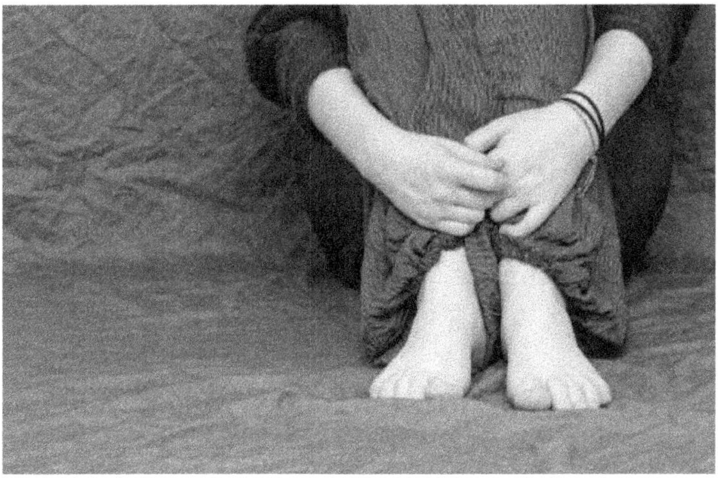

If you do find yourself on the receiving end of dark psychology with no regard for whether or not it is ethical, you may notice that you are suffering regularly. You will start to develop telltale signs of emotional abuse and manipulation. You may not be able to articulate it, but reading over this list could open your eyes to the truth. This section will go over five traits common to victims of manipulation.

You feel depressed around the manipulator

Especially if the manipulator is a partner of yours, it is common for you to feel like you are depressed or unhappy. This is because you have so much going on, even though you do not realize it. Behind the scenes, you are suffering from worsening self-esteem and confidence. Your demeanor is becoming more timid and resigned.

You feel an immense obligation to the manipulator

If you have been in a relationship of any kind with the manipulator, platonic, romantic, familial, or otherwise, you may be surprised to realize that you feel incredibly obligated to your abuser. This is often because obligation comes from manipulation, and you have been made to become obligated to the manipulator to allow for further control over you.

You have had to change to fit with your partner

This is a huge red flag—if you feel like you have changed recently, especially if other people are also commenting that you seem like you have changed recently, it is entirely possible that you have, in fact, changed, and that is problematic for everyone involved. While relationships do involve both parties bettering each other, you should never feel like you have to change to make the relationship work.

You feel like the manipulator is unpredictable

Despite potentially living with the person, you realize that you cannot predict how the manipulator will be responding to situations. They may not care about whatever has happened, or they may be incredibly frustrated about it, but you have no idea which it will be. It may seem like the other person is constantly volatile and changing, even when it is something minor.

You are constantly feeling worthless

Relationships should be full of each other, valuing each other. However, the manipulator will oftentimes completely devalue you. They want you to think that you are dumb and not worth listening to—that means that you will be complacent and easier to control. If you are too busy worrying or feeling like you do not have the self-esteem to protect or encourage your own personal growth, you may find that you actually need to get out of the relationship altogether. It is entirely possible that you have a manipulator constantly devaluing anything and everything that you do. If you do something, they immediately tell you that it does not matter or that they will not really acknowledge it even though it may have been a big deal to you.

Malicious Dark Psychology

Now, let us take one final look at what malicious dark psychology may look like. Imagine that you feel like you constantly need to be showered with lavish attention and affection. You do not know why you need it, but as long as you have lived, you have felt that desire to always be the center of attention. You will intentionally do things that gain you negative attention simply because negative attention is better than no attention, though recently, you have noticed that your partner has been feeling quite bothered by this.

Instead, you choose to change your tactics. You choose to guilt-trip your partner at every turn. You tell your partner that you do not feel appreciated and that if they had appreciated you more, then you would not be so upset. You tell your partner that you do not think that you can be in a long-term relationship with someone who is not loving enough. You lay down the guilt and threaten to leave if your partner is not more attentive to your needs, even though your partner is already struggling to spend time with you, work, and get enough sleep. You demand more and more, despite there not being much more to give.

Nevertheless, your partner desperately tries to give you more and actively attempts to spend more time with you. Your partner starts sleeping even less frequently and has a health scare. Instead of being compassionate, you continue to threaten your partner and then eventually just leave because you did not get the love you felt entitled to.

This is an example of emotional manipulation and guilt-tripping, both of which are incredibly unfair to do. The partner ends up feeling alone, heartbroken and wondering why they could not do anything right.

Notice how the partner kept trying to push his or her needs away until there was no more give. This is typical in dark psychology—the victim is often trained to feel like their own needs are problematic or should be completely foregone.

Benevolent Dark Psychology

Despite sounding kind of like an oxymoron, you can absolutely have dark psychology that has been designed to be benevolent. You could choose, for example, to make sure that whatever you are doing is meant to raise up the other party rather than dragging him or her down with you. You could make it a point to ensure that you are always honest with those around you and that you are always conscientious about people having their own opinions and free wills. No matter the form you may make sure that your influence takes, you want to ensure that it is ethical. From there, it will be a matter of judgment call for yourself.

Nevertheless, here are several situations in which dark psychology could be used to help someone:

Convincing someone to buy something that is genuinely better for them

Though it may be easier to think that people always have their own best interests in mind, that is not always the case. Sometimes, people will be on the road to making risky decisions that are going to impact them for a significant amount of time, and in those instances, you may be able to use your persuasive techniques and ability to build a rapport with ease in order to convince someone else that they are making a bad decision. For example, imagine that your friend has decided to buy a sports car for their family car. However, your friend is a single mother with custody of an infant—where will she fit the car seat? You can see that the decision does not make sense, but you cannot seem to convince your friend that she is making the wrong decision until you break out the persuasive principles to gently persuade her to do something that is in her own best interest.

Helping someone through a panic attack

As already briefly touched upon earlier, you can use body language to sort of eliminate panic attacks. However, that is not always the easiest thing to do when you are actively panicking. However, if you see a friend that is having a panic attack, it is far easier for you to go up to that friend and ask if they need any help than it would otherwise be, all because you will be able to help. You can begin to mirror your friend almost immediately and start encouraging mirroring on his end. His heart rate should slow as his breathing regulates to yours, and he should begin to calm down relatively quickly.

Presenting yourself fairly for an interview

If you are going to an interview, you may be well aware that the nerves that come along with that initial drive and walk can be incredibly intimidating. Nevertheless, knowing how best to overcome, that means that you will be able to fight off the urge to run or do something else destructive. Instead, you can use your ability to read body language and to alter your own to help you make sure that you put your best foot forward and that you could respond to the actions of your interviewer effectively.

Parenting children effectively

Children are notoriously difficult to put up with, especially during the teen years, when they think they know everything. Of course, they do not, and usually, there ends up being some sort of clash or disagreeability when trying to keep the kids on task. When this happens, however, you can always make it a point to use your ability to wield dark psychology. In this case, you may make it a point to use persuasion to really convince them that their decisions are not particularly smart and that they can make better ones, such as listening to you.

CHAPTER 4: GASLIGHTING: THE MOST DEVIOUS AND DEVASTATING PSYCHOLOGICAL ABUSE OF A MANIPULATOR

Have you ever had someone else make you feel like you were crazy? Maybe they claimed that what you were saying never really happened? When they make you doubt your mental lucidity, what you believe has happened, you can feel confused and even go so far as to fall into depression. It is a very effective mental manipulation strategy that many people employ to make others suffer and take advantage of. We are talking about "gaslighting," one of the most devious and devastating forms of abuse that exists.

The term gaslighting was not chosen at random: It is the title of a film in which the protagonist, in order to make his wife lose her mind, manages to make her believe that she is suffering from hallucinations and that she should go to a psychologist. He does all of this in order to take possession of his fortune. Real torture for those who become victims of this brutal "joke."

However, in reality, gaslighting is a form of psychological abuse.

Gaslighting: the weapon of manipulators

Although we are not used to hearing about it, the truth is that gaslighting is done much more often than it seems. It is one of the weapons of the manipulators, the one with which they can manage to drive the victim crazy until they submit to their will. Do you want some examples to understand what it is about? Perhaps they may be familiar to you.

Imagine a couple in which one partner tells the other that, during a certain conversation, the other's words hurt them. The other person says that they do not remember that discussion at all, that they are making it up, and that they would never say anything like that. Although it can always be denied, the manipulator has just planted a very important seed in his partner's head: the seed of doubt.

From that moment on, it will be a succession of episodes that will remind the victim of the moment when his partner told her that he had imagined everything and that things did not turn out that way. Faced with any such situation, the manipulator will tell her that she exaggerates, that she is lying, that her excessive sensitivity is playing tricks on her. The seed of doubt will take root, and, little by little; the victim may come to believe that she has really lost the ability to distinguish reality and imagination.

If you start constantly lying to prevent others from questioning your ideas or actions or telling you that things have turned out differently, perhaps you are victims of this kind of manipulation.

In the most extreme cases, the person who carries out this type of abuse goes so far as to hide objects and manipulate reality so that the other person thinks he or she has a misperception of things and doubts every memory of him or her. The reason why this type of abuse is perpetrated is simply to subdue the other, hurt him or her, or achieve a precise goal, as in the film Gaslighting. What is obvious is that this behavior is a clear example of a toxic relationship, in which one of the two members of the couple is overwhelmed by enormous insecurity, constant doubts about what he believes to be true, and absolute dependence on the opinion of others.

The invisible emotional manipulation: Recognizing invisible emotional manipulation so as not to be victims of it

Trust your instincts!

Is it difficult to get out of such a situation? Certainly, as happens in all cases where there is a person who wants to manipulate us. However, it is not impossible. That is why it is so important to have clear in mind the strategies that can help us to open our eyes and get out of a situation like the one described, in case we happen to be the victim of a gaslighting attempt.

The first of these strategies is to trust our intuition. When we feel that something is wrong, that things are not right, we cannot assume that the other person is right. Our instinct always speaks to us, and we must listen to it. Usually, instinct is at least as of right as the person who is trying to convince us.

The second strategy is not to seek the approval of others. This is something we always do because our self-esteem is too low or because we are dependent on the judgment of others. If our instinct, however, is already telling us that there is something strange, it is good not to give reason to those who tell us that we imagine everything.

Thirdly, it is also good to let others know how we feel and how we live in this situation. Always remember that it may well be that the other person has really forgotten about that episode and that it is not an offense to question their memories, just as it should not offend us that you question ours.

The last strategy is to clearly delimit the limits not to be crossed. If the other person screams, if he insults us or hurts us, if we notice that he is trying to use us to do what he wants us to do, we must let him know that we are not good enough and not let him pass. We cannot let someone cross the line and let them believe that they can do it with impunity; that is why we have to be decisive. If we give in once, going back will be very difficult. Any skillful psychological manipulator will take advantage of this opportunity.

Gaslighting can destroy our self-esteem, make us completely lose confidence in our common sense, cause anxiety crises, and even lead us to fall into depression.
Sometimes it is right to doubt ourselves, but in this case, it is better to look for evidence. You have to think that gaslighting

is a strategy that wants us to believe that the reality we perceive is different from the objective and concrete one. If we are convinced of this, our thoughts could become obsessive and further strengthen this idea.

Getting away from those who are hurting us is important to distance ourselves and analyze the situation from another point of view, on which there can be no manipulation. Giving reason to the other, when he makes us doubt ourselves, will give him the power to destroy us.

I want to learn not to be mistreated.

Do they see me as weak? Why me and not someone else? The mistreatment is selective, or so it seems to those who have been victims of some kind of bullying. The abuse may come from your partner, friends, or even family. The abuse can surprise us at any time and catch us completely unprepared.

The abuse can be both physical and verbal. You should always remember this detail well because verbal abuse is probably the most common, as it is the most difficult to detect. It is so veiled that, sometimes, we cannot understand who our aggressors are because their violence lies in their words.

"The difference between aggression and maltreatment is defined by the objective of the action. Aggression is defined by the injury it causes, while maltreatment is described with words like submission, humiliation, domination, fear, slavery, etc.."

Learning to be assertive

The first thing you need to understand if you don't want to be mistreated is that you need to learn to be assertive. Assertion is a quality that you can learn. Learn to assert your rights, learn to be respected, learn to express your feelings...

It's very easy to say, but more difficult to do, and the attacker knows this well. For this reason, always try to take advantage of situations that leave you completely open-mouthed, it surprises you! In this way, you will not know how to react. Until such a situation is repeated a second time, you will not know which way to turn. You feel confused, sometimes even lost, and you are so surprised by the actions of the attacker that you are almost in a state of shock. This is completely normal. Sometimes the situation is bigger than you. Different and varied situations that you never expected to happen, let alone at the hands of that person!

"In maltreatment", the effect triggered is much greater than the physical cause.

At this point, it is necessary to reflect on the following question: will you respond or react to the abuse? They are two very different things. Remember that the important thing is not to get into the aggressor's game; what you have to achieve is that he stops caring about you.

To stop being interesting for the aggressor, you need to know how to fight back in front of everything he tells you. This is what the assertion is for. The best thing you can do is not to let someone use their power against you, do not let them intimidate you.

Do not play the aggressor's game

As we have already said, the best thing to do is not to play his game. That's why your reaction is very important because that's how the attacker will know whether to leave you alone or continue. In this regard, here are some factors to take into account and that will help you to fight against an aggressor:

- The aggressor will create fear in you. Use it to think quickly, to stay awake, and to know how to respond. Do not allow fear to paralyze or fail you.

- Be convinced and doubt all the orders given by the aggressor. Do not let him know that he has power over you. Who is he to give you orders?

- Be sure of yourself. Self-confidence is something palpable and keeps away any aggressor who is looking for a victim.

- Don't be aggressive because then you will get into his game. The important thing is not to be too submissive or too aggressive. A balance between the two is the best thing.

- Non-verbal language betrays. Stay calm, look the other one in the eye, and keep your gaze fixed. It is very important that your voice does not tremble and that you are confident at all times.

It is true that there are people who are more exposed to abuse than others. For example, there are some people who oppose verbal abuse and, for this reason, become victims of physical assaults. It is something that is always talked about, but then, out of fear, few act. If you think you are not able to prevent abuse, seek help! There are people who can help and support you. You are not alone.

"Psychological abuse is what completely destroys the victim, as well as torment, feeling controlled, not feeling loved. Silence, a cold look or a contemptuous look also hurt a lot."

Emotionally strong people: 7 distinctive features

The traits that distinguish emotionally strong people have nothing to do with character hardness or inflexibility or a tendency to impose themselves on others. On the contrary, emotional strength is not expressed through gestures of strength, but mainly through resistance and self-control.

The characteristics common to emotionally strong people are, therefore, associated with the concept of moderation and balance. We come into the world without one and without the other, but we can potentially develop both. It depends on each of us to nurture them.

Self-control is, therefore, the keyword. This has nothing to do with the repression of feelings but with the ability to filter what we feel so that it does not "explode," leading us to act in a way that damages ourselves and others. Emotionally strong personality traits speak to us precisely of self-control. Here are 7.

Traits of emotionally strong people

1. **Do not try to attract attention:** One of the characteristics of emotionally strong people is that they are esteemed. This means that they do not depend on other people's opinions to think or feel that what they say has value and makes sense. They let themselves be guided by themselves.

On the contrary, one of the characteristics of emotional fragility is over-dependence on other people's opinions. This means that they do not value themselves enough and give others control over their lives.

2. **Resilience:** This feature is strongly related to the previous one. One of the typical traits of emotional strength is the ability to deal with rejection and manage it without it hurting, leaving scars, or affecting one's actions.
Clearly, it hurts any of us to receive a rejection. However, when being rejected triggers excessive fear, we end up saying "yes" when we would like to say "no" only for fear that others

will exclude us or question us. We are endowed with emotional strength when we face this fear and learn to handle it in the right way.

3. **They do what they want:** Doing what you want does not mean acting arbitrarily and capriciously, as a child does. The "will" typical of childhood is different from that of the adult. In the first case, it is the result of an impulse; in the second, it is the result of deep self-knowledge and self-control.
An emotionally strong person is able to decide what he wants after a process of reflection. He also has enough will to pursue what he wants and not let go.

4. **Do not try to harm others:** The desire to harm others arises only when there is something indefinite or unresolved inside us. In any circumstance, human beings need each other; this is because we are interdependent beings.
An emotionally healthy person knows this and therefore sees others as his or her peers. He respects them and gives them a certain value, just as he claims to be respected and valued in turn. He knows that cooperation and understanding are ways to achieve a life full of satisfaction.

5. **They choose their friendships:** One of the traits of emotionally strong people is that they are selective with those

they let into their lives. They know they cannot open the doors of their hearts completely to anyone.
They also understand that a part of their well-being depends on the quality of the relationships they have with others. For this reason, they reject stifling, conflictual, or weary bonds. Conversely, they seek healthy relationships.

6. **They are not afraid of change:** Not being afraid of change is an unequivocal sign of emotional strength. If we are, or if we feel fragile, the normal thing is to try to follow our routine religiously so that we feel safe. In this way, we feel protected, however much this deprives us of a full life.
When we perceive ourselves as emotionally strong people, there is a desire to explore, to change. This is why we seek new experiences. Everything that is new usually produces a kind of fear, but in some moments of our lives, it is also the only way to move forward.

7. **Not Influential:** An emotionally strong person questions the information they receive. Before accepting it as true, he analyzes and evaluates it. He is not attentive to fashion trends or the physical or mental trends of the moment.

Obviously, this requires enough self-confidence. But, above all, it requires each of us to know what is best for ourselves.

For this reason, everything that is chosen and followed by the majority becomes an object of examination.

Those listed are just a few typical traits of emotionally strong people. We have chosen a list to simplify a really complex reality. The important thing is not to understand if you fall into the category but to take this information as a point of reference for constructive self-criticism.

Learn the ten things that mentally strong people do every day

Learn to say "no," learn to know what you want, what you don't want to allow, what you deserve... Your self-confidence frightens attackers. High self-esteem and unbreakable security will be your best weapons to make the aggressors flee and prevent them from approaching you.

Surely you will know people who are mentally strong and others who are mentally weak. However, have you ever wondered what it really means? A mentally strong person is, for example, the one who is not influenced by others, who you know, and who is proud of his personality. A mentally strong person knows themselves and does not allow anyone to change themselves.

Maybe you don't know if you are a strong person or not, or maybe you are looking for a way to become one. Today we will tell you about ten things that mentally strong people do every day. We hope they will help you become such!

Remember that the strongest branches grow in a headwind.

1. **They know how to say "no.":** A difficult thing for many because they taught us to always say "yes" because otherwise we will be considered rude and unpleasant people. Our yearning for approval always pushes us to say "yes."
You must learn that saying "no" is not a bad thing because you have every right to refuse to do or accept something you do not want. If it is difficult for you to say "no," how about trying today to stop doing what you do not want to do?

2. **Accept failures:** Mentally strong people know that every failure brings with it an experience and that an experience is a new way to know what we have done well, what we have not done, and what we must do to move forward.
There is no success without failure; without failure, we get tired; without failure, we trust ourselves too much, and we may reach our goal, realizing that what we did was not as good or not as we hoped.

Sometimes success is the deepest failure. Don't complain before your time. Have confidence.

3. **Their happiness does not depend on others:** We believe that in order to be happy, others must be happy too, and even worse, that our happiness always depends on others. This is a serious mistake. Your happiness is yours alone, and if you allow it to depend on others, you will see yourself overwhelmed by a come-and-go of emotions that will only make you feel unhappy and frustrated. Happiness is within you. You still don't understand it? Look for it!

4. **Draw positive lessons from negative events:** We must not dramatize; in this life, we always give too much importance to all the negative events that happen to us. However, are they really negative? Mentally strong people know that something positive can always be drawn from any negative event. That something is right there, but you cannot see it. Open your eyes to negative things you learn, and thanks to them, you move on.
To see the rainbow, first, you will have to face the rain.

5. **Face fears:** They know that fear is also an emotion, which paralyzes if we allow it to invade us. That's why mentally strong people face fear and use it to their advantage. Through

it, they face and overcome all the aspects they fear; they put themselves to the test! And so they become strong, mentally powerful.

6. **They are emotionally intelligent:** There are few emotionally intelligent people who understand and identify emotions, which is an extremely difficult process. They are people with a high empathic capacity. And you, can you control your emotions? Can you identify and use them to your advantage? If the answer is yes, then you are emotionally intelligent. Emotionally intelligent people know how to express their emotions.

7. **They trust in their abilities:** We are human, and at any time, our trust can be questioned or destroyed. Are you sure you can do what you would like? Emotionally intelligent people always trust themselves and do not allow anything or anyone to crush their trust. Self-confidence is important if you want to be strong.

8. **Neutralize toxic people:** Toxic people surround us and sometimes turn us into who we don't want to be. If you are emotionally strong, you will know how to neutralize toxic people.

You just need to believe in yourself, find the strength and pride you need to move away from these people and face them if necessary. Do not be overwhelmed by toxic people. Darkness and negativity are places where no one likes to be. Some people are like clouds; when they leave, the days begin to be serene again.

9. **Accept the changes:** Because sometimes you are afraid of change, of leaving the comfort zone! However, mentally strong people know that any change is positive. Open your eyes, accept change, accept to be mentally strong people.

10. **They know that the world owes them nothing**

Sometimes we believe that the world is in our debt, that if we do something good, something good will come back to us. Do not take anything for granted and do not want too many things. Look around you; what do you have? Be happy with what you have now; appreciate it, value it. It is in these details that you will find the true happiness and strength that you seek so much.

Sometimes we believe that we have nothing, but this happens only because we do not know how to look at and appreciate what surrounds us.

So, do you identify yourself in these ten aspects that characterize mentally strong people? If the answer is yes, congratulations! And if the answer is no, now you know what you have to do! Start now to change your vision of things, of the world, of reality. Life is full of wonderful things, and you are mentally strong; you just don't know it yet. There are cruel individuals disguised as good people...

Who are cruel individuals disguised as good people

They are beings who hurt, who attack through machiavellian emotional blackmail based on fear, aggression, and guilt. They show spectacular goodness behind which hidden interests and deep frustrations are hidden.

It is often said that those who hurt do so because they have been hurt in turn. Who has been offended, offends others. These ideas do not have a truthful basis. Moreover, there is another aspect to consider and that we do not always like to admit. Wickedness exists. Cruel people sometimes have certain biological characteristics that lead them to adopt aggressive behavior.

"There is no evil more cruel than that which is born from the seeds of good."

The Argentine scholar and popularizer, Marcelino Cereijido, points out an interesting aspect. "There is no evil gene, but some biological and cultural circumstances that can favor it." The most complex aspect is that, very often, we tend to put labels and pathologies on behaviors that simply do not fit in the psychodiagnostic manuals.

Evil actions can occur without the necessary presence of an underlying psychological illness. All of us, at some time in our lives, have known a person with this profile. Beings who treat us with flattery and attention. Nice people, well seen by society, but who in private outline a dark and very elongated shadow. In the abyss of their hearts reside cruelty, lack of empathy, and even aggressiveness.
We propose that you reflect on this theme.

Cruel people and the molecule of morality

As we have indicated, no one today has been able to affirm the existence of the evil gene. In any case, in recent years, studies on a fascinating aspect have increased: the so-called "molecule of morality." To better understand what it is, we present a true story, a terrible story that, unfortunately, occurs too frequently.

Hans Reiser is an American programmer famous for creating ReiserFS files. Since 2008 he has been in Mule Creek prison for killing his wife. He had no qualms about pleading guilty and revealing where he buried Nina Reiser's body. It should be noted that this programming specialist has a prodigious intelligence, so much so that he began his university studies when he was just a teenager.

After a quick trial and being detained in San Quintín prison, he decided to prepare his appeal himself. Using five handwritten sheets of paper, he declared that his brain worked differently. Reiser was aware of the oxytocin studies that were being carried out at the time and used them as a defense argument. According to him, he was born with this problem: his brain did not produce the so-called morality molecule; it was therefore devoid of empathy.

Obviously, as expected, this statement did not exempt him from serving life imprisonment. However, the debate on the origin of evil reopened. Nowadays, full value is given to the theory that oxytocin is the hormone that makes us be "human" in its most authentic meaning: people who respect and care for, care for, and empathize with their fellow human beings.

How to defend yourself against camouflaged cruelty

In our daily life, we do not always relate to cruel people like the one just described. However, we are victims of other types of interactions: those of false goodness, hidden aggression, manipulation, subtle selfishness, the most harmful irony, etc..

"The world is a dangerous place, not because of those who do evil deeds but for those who observe without saying anything."

-Albert Einstein-

These behaviors can be the result of several factors. Lack of emotional intelligence, a lack of affectionate environment in which the person grew up, and, why not, a deficit of oxytocin. All this, perhaps, can determine a more or less hidden aggressiveness. In any case, we cannot forget that with aggressiveness, we are not referring only to physical abuse.

Emotional, instrumental, or verbal aggression inflicts wounds less visible but more frequent, and we must defend ourselves against them. We explain how.

Cruel people: knowing how to recognize and avoid them

Everyone can be a victim of cruel people. No matter the age, status, or previous experiences. These profiles are present in the family, at work, or in any other scenario. However, we can identify them in different ways.

- The person with a dark heart will conquer us with lies. They will dress up in beautiful words and noble actions, but little by little, they will use blackmail. Later, fear, guilt, and mental violence.

- Faced with these mechanisms, there is only one option: do not tolerate. It does not matter whether it is our sister, our partner, or a colleague. Those who disturb our soul and our balance want only one thing: to turn off our self-esteem in order to have control over us.

- We will have the clear feeling that there is no way out that we are under their clutches. However, we must remember that it is more powerful who is master of himself. You have to break the game of control and aggressiveness with force.
The games of control and hidden aggression are very intricate. In any case, it is necessary to act quickly by dismantling the traps and reacting to veiled threats. When

we feel uneasiness or anxiety about certain behaviors, there is only one option: distance.

CHAPTER 5: STAYING FREE

Once you are finally out of the relationship, you may find that after some time, you miss it. You will miss your ex, and while he may have been abusive or threatening, you still spent a portion of your life with him and feel like you want that back. It is only natural to miss those that you care about, but ultimately, you must have the self-confidence and self-discipline to remind yourself that you made the right decision to leave.

In particular, you may find that you miss the good times, and that is natural. If your relationship had been nothing but negative, it never would have progressed beyond the initial date—the narcissist had to be able to win you over somehow, and that usually involves some sort of façade and persona. Nevertheless, it can be incredibly difficult to avoid the feelings of wanting to go back to the abuser, even after you have finally escaped once and for all.

Keep in mind that if you have just escaped your relationship and feel like you want to go back, you are not alone. On average, it takes at least seven attempts for a person to break free from an abusive partner. However, just because wanting to go back and knowing that other people regularly go back does not mean that you should simply decide to go back because you miss your ex—you should try to resist. Retain that freedom that you fought for so hard and make sure that you stay free.

In particular, this chapter will take the time to provide you with some advice designed to help keep you from returning to your abusive situation despite the temptation and desire you may have to do exactly that. Even if you are depressed where you are, or feeling like your home would be better than the room in a shelter that you are in, resist. Any time that you feel like you are wishing that things were different or when you tell yourself that you are struggling due to your own failures, remind yourself that abuse is not your fault. It is not your fault that you were targeted by a narcissist. You were preyed upon by the abuser, and that had nothing to do with who you are or what you deserve. You could never have known that everything would play out the way that they did. That is not your fault, and it never will be.

The road to recovery begins with you no longer taking blame for the narcissist's actions. This means that you must reject the idea that you are somehow at fault for everything that happened. The abuse lies firmly with the narcissist, and you need to remind yourself of that. Remind yourself that no one deserves to be abused in your moments of weakness, and remind yourself that you may not be where you had hoped to be, but at least you are free. You have left that cage once and for all and you are finally free to stretch your wings and learn to fly.

Now that you are away, it is time to stay away. You can do it.

Find Support

The first way that can help you strengthen your resolve during those moments of weakness is to find support. Find friends or family that you can turn to if you need to talk during those moments, knowing that you will be fully and wholly supported by them when you do so. Make sure that you primarily surround yourself with people that you know and trust, or find a support group for people with similar stories to you.

If you have gone through a domestic violence shelter, you may already have access to this by having access to all of the resources that usually follow the shelter. They likely have support groups held for those living at the shelter at any given time. If they do not have a support group, they can surely point you in the right direction toward finding one that will be beneficial to you.

You are very likely to find that being able to talk to other people will actually be incredibly beneficial to you—when you can talk to others, you are free to hear other stories .Just knowing that other people have lived through what you have been through can help you find comfort in those moments of loneliness when you are wondering where you went so wrong. You will be able to branch out and make new friends who have been where you are. They will know how to help you simply because they will have been there before, and their advice can be absolutely critical to keeping you afloat during such a dark time.

Write Down Your Reasons for Leaving

Another way that may help you fight off all of the tempting feelings of going back to the narcissist is to write down every reason that you left. Spend the time when you are safe to go over what made you finally pull the trigger and leave. For Talia, it was that the Ned she knew was a lie. She did not appreciate being fooled into falling in love for someone who never existed in the first place. For you, it could be that you are sick of the abuse. You finally acknowledge that you deserve better, or that your children deserve better.

If you do have children, look at them. Do they deserve to grow up in a home full of dysfunction? Do you really want that life for them? Most parents would never want that for their children, and for them, leaving would be the obvious choice.

Of course, just because you know that you would want better for your children does not mean that your feelings will just stop. Your feelings are just that—feelings—, and they are not to be believed.

After having written down all of the reasons that you can think of for leaving, you can return to the list any time that you are feeling week. Are you thinking about that one date that you had that was entirely romantic, next to the beach? Remind yourself that it was probably a lie and that the narcissist most likely felt nothing for you and read over your list. Are you realizing that your birthday is coming up, and you are going to have to spend it without an adult to talk to? Read over that list again and remind yourself why it is so important to you.

Consider also writing down any and all instances of suspected gaslighting that you can think of. Think about all the times that your ex told you something was wrong or that you were not remembering things properly. Think of how you felt, feeling like you were slowly losing your mind, and latch onto that anger. Tell yourself that you are not going to accept that treatment again, and you are not willing to return to being treated like you cannot possibly understand what is right in front of your face.

Find a Hobby

Perhaps one of the least specific pieces of advice that you are ever going to receive consider finding a hobby or something else to keep you busy during moments of weakness. Just having something else to do to occupy the time can help the feeling pass, even when you are feeling tempted to return back to the narcissist for any reason at all.

Have you ever wanted to try something new or learn a new skill? This is the time to go for it—figure out exactly what it is that you have been wanting in life and go for it. If you have always dreamed of learning to draw without being mocked or laughed at for whatever you have chosen as your medium or subject, now is your time. Do you want to make it a point to learn how to knit? Take some extra cash if you have it and go get a beginner's kit. You have nothing but time on your hands that used to be filled by the narcissist—take it back and do something for yourself.

This does two things: Not only are you keeping yourself busy, but you are also doing something to better yourself, and bettering yourself may help you feel better about yourself. Boosting your self-confidence as you succeed at a new skill is always a huge welcome bonus.

CHAPTER 6: WHAT IS EMPATHY ONE?

Empathy: the pleasure of emotional reading for the brain

Empathy is the ability of our emotional brain to read or perceive the thoughts and feelings of others. How does it work?

Empathy: the art of understanding emotions

We could define empathy as the ability to put on the shoes of others, to understand their world view, their point of view, and their opinions, without prejudice.

Empathy is not only useful for others, but it is also useful for ourselves.

"The ability to put ourselves in the shoes of others is one of the most important functions of intelligence. It shows the degree of maturity of the human being."

What is empathy, and what is it for?

Empathy is the ability to put oneself in other people's shoes, to understand them, to try to understand what is going on in their mind, as it is because they feel in a certain way, but not from their own point of view, but trying to think like them, with their ideas, their values...

Empathy starts from valuing, from understanding that a person's feelings are possible in the situation they are in, even if we, in the same situation, would think differently.

Put simply, and with an example, perhaps it is not so important for us to be an only child, but for another person, it can be. In this case, the empathetic person knows how to put aside his "scale of the importance of things" to understand the suffering of the other according to "his scale of the importance of things."

The degree of empathy

There are people to be empathetic comes naturally, but others are completely incapable of doing so. Nevertheless, be careful!
Sometimes we confuse empathy with another concept that, although it is not the same, is very important to be empathetic. We are talking about the ability to recognize emotions.

It is about being able to recognize sadness, happiness, fear, or anger. There are people who can quickly capture the emotional state of a person, while others who would not be able to even if they had written it on their foreheads, to exaggerate a bit.

Obviously, there are many factors that affect this phase that precedes the more cognitive part of empathy: the familiarity you have with the other person, our level of fatigue, his or her communicative predisposition, etc.

Empathy involves many positive aspects: it facilitates communication, consolation, problem-solving, etc.. However, there is also the opposite extreme, the negative one.

Living always adopting a point of view that is not ours can be the cause of an emotional disconnection with ourselves, which could cost us dearly.
For this reason, we advise you to practice and train your mental capacity to put yourself in other people's shoes, but without forgetting that this is not about yourself and not staying there forever. The first ones who have to take care of us are ourselves.

When do we show our empathy?

It is possible to be a very empathetic person, but if we are not able to demonstrate it, if we do not put it into practice, it is useless. Having said that, we want to list some situations in which we use this ability:

- When we can listen and understand the feelings of others without caring about ourselves or our own words.

- When we do not only use words to console others. A hug, hand on shoulder, kiss, or caress also makes us more empathetic.

- When we are with someone who has a problem and, for example, we also help them with their sense of humor.

- When we can express ourselves gently and courteously.

- When we do not show gestures of boredom, irritation, or tiredness at what they are telling us.

- When we do not make a comment, joke, or joke, if we know they will bother the other.

- When, for example, we make an elderly person or a child understand that we understand them.

- When we help someone to solve a problem and are able to calm others.
When do we not show our empathy?

On the contrary, there are also times and situations when we do not show our empathy:

- When we think that our problems are the only important ones.
- When we do not listen to others.
- When we judge and make inappropriate comments.
- When we never offer a smile, a kind gesture, or a caress to others.
- Whenever we do something for others, we expect something in return.

Empathy is an excellent skill to put into practice, as it allows us to better understand others. However, we must be careful and not use it too much to avoid losing the bond with ourselves.

Empathy: the pleasure of emotional reading for the brain

Empathy is the ability of our emotional brain to read or perceive the thoughts and feelings of others. Developing it means perceiving others' emotions as if they were our own, understanding their psyche, and being able to provide them with the support or support they need.

It is not easy to reconstruct the exact map of all one's own and others' emotions, but it is worth a try. The result will be a solid push to positively strengthen the bonds we will weave in the future, our ability to reach out to others, and the joy that will be generated in us as a result of generosity.

Because being able to wear the clothes of sadness of another person, for example, shows the incredible ability to express one's emotional capacity with courage and intelligence.

Contrary to what you might think, considering that the term emotional capacity has now become part of the common language, it is not so easy to reach or obtain it. However, the fact that we are emotional beings who learn to think, not thinking machines who learn to feel, plays in our favor. Even if we often do not remember it.

"True empathic listeners can even hear what is said in silence. The most important aspect of communication is to hear what is not being said."

Emotional learning: the basis for empathy development

Our first contacts with emotions instruct us on what to look at and what to ignore in the world of feelings and emotions. Emotional learning consists of several premises:

- The first step towards empathic learning is to strive to be able to perceive the emotions of others. In other words, we have to tune into the feelings and emotions of others so that we can understand their inner world.

- The second learning strongly argues that acting with empathy does not mean adopting the perspective of others but looking at the world with different eyes. This helps us to understand why a person is acting in a certain way.

- Empathic understanding encapsulates an emotional response to the person in question, aimed at trying to understand the reasons that lead them to certain feelings and actions.

- It is also good to know that it is not just about perceiving and understanding what the other person feels but that they feel understood. In this way, the circle will be closed, and the benefits of being empathetic will become evident.

It is, therefore, a matter of coordinating actions on a cognitive, behavioral, and sentimental level. It is good to be able to differentiate between the concept of empathy and sympathy: thanks to the latter, it is possible to perceive the feelings of others, but not to the point of understanding them.

Empathy involves understanding and feeling other people's emotional states as if they were your own. In order to achieve a sensitivity that captures non-verbal messages, practice is needed, just like a mathematical equation or a syntactical analysis.

Empathy: the emotional reading of our brain

If we are well disposed, we will be able to reach the emotional state that will allow us to capture the harmony and decipher the desires, dreams, messages hidden deep inside, the needs ... This process, so incredible that it can seem magical, happens inside our brain, which is able to read skillfully and intensely every emotion.

The next question to ask is, of course, how it does this. Fortunately, science has been investigating such issues for years and has come to identify the many areas in which our emotional capacity resides. Let's discover some of them together:

- One of the most important discoveries in the field of neuroscience is that of mirror neurons, present within our emotional circuits. They are brain cells with the task of reflecting in the brain everything we observe (no need to emphasize what it feels like when you see someone yawning).

- The limbic system is the basis of our emotional brain. This area of the brain is active from birth, even inside the maternal uterus. It includes the temporal lobe, the amygdala, the hippocampus, and the orbitofrontal cortex, which has the function of distributing information about one's own and others' moods, channeling it, and transmitting it to the rest of the body.

- The frontal lobe is the executive center of our brain. This part is in charge of shaping and managing the emotions of the limbic system in order to insert them into the environment around us. In other words, it is the area that allows us to have a functional role in society, allowing us to act correctly according to social norms, as well as to be reflective of our feelings and actions.

- The cerebral hemispheres. In general terms, it can be said that the left hemisphere dominates the ability to reflect on emotions, while the right hemisphere is more concerned with the limbic system.

Although the brain differences can be abysmal from individual to individual, it has been seen that in men, executive brain activity dominates over emotions, while in women, the limbic system prevails. These data seem to confirm the commonplace that women show greater empathic abilities.

In any case, empathy can be developed in men as well as in women on equal terms. It is, therefore, important to put an order in your emotional brain and strive to look at the world with external eyes. The journey will be wonderful.

Empathy: the art of understanding emotions

We could define empathy as the ability to put on the shoes of others, to understand their world view, their point of view, and their opinions, without prejudice.

Empathy is not only useful for others, but it is also useful for ourselves.

"The ability to put ourselves in the shoes of others is one of the most important functions of intelligence. It shows the degree of maturity of the human being."

Empathy implies many positive aspects: it facilitates communication, consolation, problem-solving, etc.. However, there is also the opposite extreme, the negative one.

Living always adopting a point of view that is not ours can be the cause of an emotional disconnection with ourselves, which could cost us dearly.

For this reason, we advise you to practice and train your mental capacity to put yourself in other people's shoes, but without forgetting that this is not about yourself and not staying there forever. The first ones who have to take care of us are ourselves.

When do we show our empathy?

It is possible to be a very empathetic person, but if we are not able to demonstrate it, if we do not put it into practice, it is useless. Having said that, we want to list some situations in which we use this ability:

- When we can listen and understand the feelings of others without caring about ourselves or our own words.
- When we do not only use words to console others. A hug, hand on shoulder, kiss, or caress also makes us more empathetic.
- When we are with someone who has a problem and, for example, we also help them with their sense of humor.
- When we can express ourselves gently and courteously.
- When we do not show gestures of boredom, irritation, or tiredness at what they are telling us.
- When we do not make a comment, joke, or joke, if we know they will bother the other.
- When, for example, we make an elderly person or a child understand that we understand them.
- When we help someone to solve a problem and are able to calm others.

When do we not show our empathy?

On the contrary, there are also moments and situations in which we do not show our empathy:

- When we think that our problems are the only important ones.

- When we do not listen to others.
- When we judge and make inappropriate comments.
- When we never offer a smile, a kind gesture, or a caress to others.
- Whenever we do something for others, we expect something in return.

Empathy is an excellent skill to put into practice, as it allows us to better understand others. However, we must be careful and not use it too much to avoid losing the bond with ourselves.

CONCLUSION

Congratulations! That brings us to the end of ***Dark Psychology***. Hopefully, as you read, you found the content to be compelling, interesting, informative, and easy to follow. With care, this book was designed to guide you through the world of dark psychology.

Dark psychology is the look into the minds of the most heinous, monstrous humans that exist. When you are looking into the depths of dark psychology, you are looking into the minds of those who are out to hurt others. Serial killers, master manipulators, and abusers alike may share these traits, and those traits make them particularly dangerous. What is worse, however, is that these people understand psychology. They understand exactly how they need to interact with other people in order to be seen as charismatic and trustworthy enough to win a spot in the hearts of their victims and targets. The dark psychology user is able to do this simply by knowing how to manipulate their target in just the right way.

However, they can only hurt and manipulate you if you give them that power. Remember, having the power to recognize and reject the abuse from the dark psychology user will be your best shield and sword from them. Not only will it help you guard against them and their attempts, you will also be able to access their minds right back.

As you read through this book, perhaps the most important takeaway from it all is to remember that dark psychology itself is neutral—it is neither good nor bad. While the original wielders may have been malevolent, that does not make their weapons inherently bad as well. Remember that being able to understand dark psychology grants you a special access to the mind of someone else and you should always be mindful of how you use that access. It should not be abused in any manner.

Finally, as you finish up, remember to always keep your own use of dark psychology ethical. Always ask yourself if you really need to tap into the mind of someone else. Ask yourself if the other person is the primary beneficiary if you do happen to tap into their mind. Ask yourself if they will be happy to have the end results of you tapping into their mind. If you can answer that they will be benefitted significantly and they will appreciate it, then it may be an acceptable time to use your arts.

Nevertheless, as this book draws to a close, you may be wondering what comes next. Ultimately, that depends upon you. You have learned some of the basics of dark psychology. Do you want to learn more about the natural users? Do you want to learn how to fight it? Do you want to learn how to become a better user? What is your end goal?

No matter what that goal is, you may find that there are several options for you to pursue from here. You could make it a point to learn how to become emotionally intelligent. This goes hand-in-hand with being able to persuade others with ease. You may decide to look into the process of cognitive behavioral therapy—doing so may provide you with more resources to protect yourself and heal from any manipulation that you may have identified in your life. You may decide that what is right for you is to look into the narcissist himself, learning how he abuses in order to better understand him. You may even choose to delve into psychology in general—there are several different topics that you may find to be interesting and useful in your journey from here on out.

No matter what you choose, however, keep in mind that it is up to you.l No matter what anyone else tries to convince you, you deserve free will. You deserve to be able to protect that free will. You deserve to have that free will honored. As you go through the next chapter in your journey, good luck. Hopefully, you have found what you needed within this book, and you will find what you need in the future as well.

CPSIA information can be obtained
at www.ICGtesting.com
Printed in the USA
BVHW061912250321
603415BV00014B/1903

9 781802 250121